My name is

· ·

Note to Parents and Teachers

This book is a very first introduction to weather. The lively illustrations show the differences between basic types of weather (sunny, cloudy, rainy, snowy etc.) in the clearest and most unambiguous way, giving young children a good understanding of this topic.

Oxford University Press, Great Clarendon Street, Oxford OX2 6DP

Oxford is a trade mark of Oxford University Press
Copyright © Oxford University Press 1999
First published 1999
3 5 7 9 10 8 6 4

A CIP catalogue record for this book is available from the British Library

ISBN 0-19-910546-4 (hardback)
ISBN 0-19-910547-2 (paperback)

Printed in Hong Kong by OUP Hong Kong

My first book of Weather

Illustrated by Julie Park

Consultant: Peter Patilla

Oxford University Press

sunny

very sunny

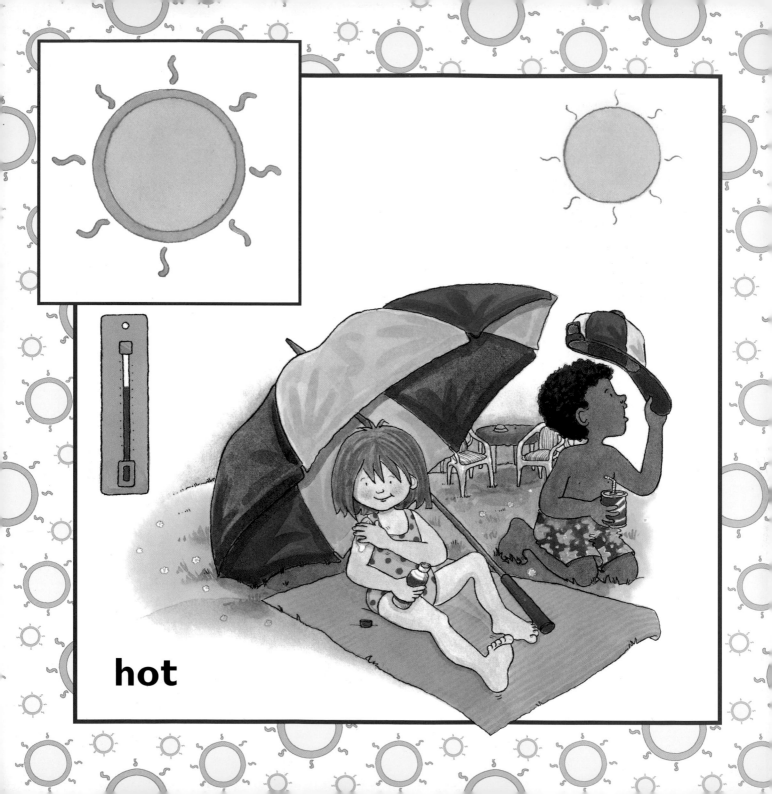

hot

very hot

windy

very windy

cloudy

very cloudy

foggy

very foggy

rainy

very rainy

stormy

very stormy

cold

very cold

snowy

very snowy

Can you. . .

name the colours of the rainbow?

What's the weather like when

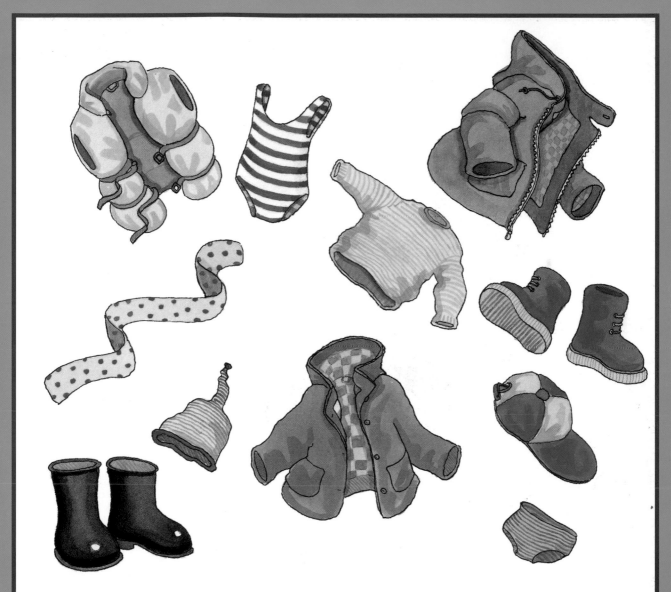

you wear these clothes?

What do these weather

symbols mean?